# Dams Give Us Power

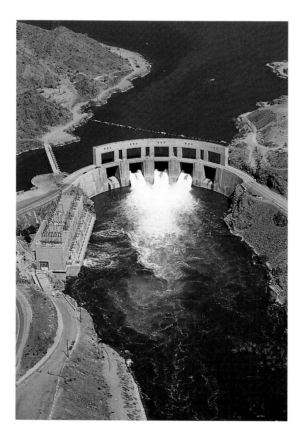

# Dams Give Us Power

a building block book

Lee Sullivan Hill

Carolrhoda Books, Inc./Minneapolis

*For my father, Philip R. Sullivan. WHaHF.*
*—Love, Lee*

For metric conversion, when you know the number of miles, multiply by 1.61 to find the number of kilometers. When you know the number of feet, multiply by 30 to find the number of centimeters. When you know the number of gallons, multiply by 3.8 to find the number of liters. And when you know the number of acres, multiply by .4 to find the number of hectares.

The photographs in this book are reproduced through the courtesy of: © D. J. Lambrecht, front cover; © Betty Crowell, back cover, pp. 11, 21; © S. Strickland/Naturescapes, pp. 1, 24; © Erwin C. "Bud" Nielsen, "Images International," p. 2; © Root Resources/Mary Root, p. 5; © David Jensen, pp. 6, 29; © Jack Olson, p. 7; © Diane C. Lyell, p. 8; © Thomas R. Fletcher, p. 9; © Hutchinson Library, pp. 10, 22; © Visuals Unlimited, pp. 12 (Tom Edwards), 14 (Dick Poe); © Frank L. Lambrecht, p. 13; © Jo-Ann M. Ordano, pp. 15, 16; © Jim Yuskavitch, pp. 17, 18, 26, 28; © Glenn Randall, pp. 19, 25; *Deseret News* photo by Tom Smart, p. 20; © Gene Boaz, p. 23; © Bob Firth, p. 27.

Text copyright © 1997 by Lee Sullivan Hill

Carolrhoda Books, Inc. c/o The Lerner Publishing Group
241 First Avenue North, Minneapolis, MN 55401 U.S.A.


Library of Congress Cataloging-in-Publication Data

Hill, Lee Sullivan, 1958–
Dams give us power / by Lee Sullivan Hill.
     p. cm. — (A building block book)
    Includes index.
    Summary: Introduces readers to dams, their purposes, and how they may be built.
    ISBN 1-57505-023-4
    1. Dams—Juvenile literature. [1. Dams.] I. Title. II. Series: Hill, Lee Sullivan, 1958–
Building block book.
TC540.H47  1997
627'.8—dc20                                                                        96–8570

Manufactured in the United States of America
1 2 3 4 5 6 – SP – 02 01 00 99 98 97

Dams hold back water.

Some dams are small. Take a look at a
beaver dam. Sticks and mud slow down the
stream. Water pools behind the jumble-jam.
A new pond is born.

Some dams are big.  The Glen Canyon Dam
in Arizona stands over 700 feet tall.  Its concrete
wall holds back a river.

Dams can make waterfalls. A smooth stream slips over the top of a dam. It crashes to the bottom and bubbles away downstream.

Some dams are just for fun. Kids piled up rocks to make this shady swimming hole.

Fish swim at the bottom.  Water bugs whisk across the top. YIKES!  The water is cold.

People build dams to bring water to dry places. Ancient Egyptians built dams on the Nile River thousands of years ago. The dams helped people grow food in the desert.

Modern Egyptians built the Aswan High Dam in the 1960s. It stores water in a reservoir that's 300 miles long.

Hoover Dam in Nevada stores water in its reservoir, Lake Mead. Each spring, rain and melted snow swell the Colorado River. Hoover Dam saves this water to use in the dry summers.

Water from Lake Mead travels to Arizona and California. It may not rain for weeks in summer, but people in Los Angeles can still get a drink of water. Farmers can water their crops. Firefighters can put out fires.

Back at Lake Mead, people can go boating, swimming, and fishing. Dams hold back water for many people to use.

Dams can store water to make power. The ancient Romans dammed streams. They used the power of water to turn wheels.

Americans use water wheels, too. This old mill still grinds wheat into flour.

The Bonneville Dam on the Columbia River stores water for electric power. Pipes carry water through the dam to a powerhouse.

Once inside the powerhouse, water pushes turbines around and around. This water power makes electricity. Pipes under each turbine catch the water and return it to the river.

All along the Columbia River, people use dams to bring water to crops. They use power from dams to turn on the lights.

When dams are built, fish need help moving up and down rivers. Pike, salmon, and trout travel around some dams on water steps called fish ladders.

People study fish in the rivers and lakes near dams. They measure and weigh fish to be sure they are healthy.

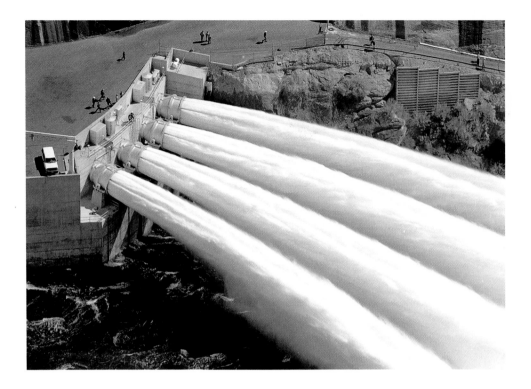

At the Glen Canyon Dam, some fish were sick.
Spring floods had not cleaned the river since the
dam was built. Weeds clogged the water.

To help the fish, scientists made a spring
flood. Water gushed past the open gates in the
dam. After the flood, the river was clean.

Many dams help stop floods. Water from the Chang River in China used to flow over the banks. Floods swept away houses and roads. Now dams hold back floodwaters. Gates let water out bit by bit.

Very long dams, called barriers, protect some cities. The Thames River Barrier keeps London, England, safe. In high water, steel gates rise up from the riverbed. When the water goes back down, only the gateposts can be seen.

Engineers design barriers and dams.
They measure how much water runs in a river.
They test the dirt and rocks that will hold up the
dam.  And they study which kind of dam will
work best.

If there is plenty of good dirt and rock nearby,
engineers might plan an earthen dam.

They might plan a masonry dam, with stones stacked one on top of the other. Or they might decide that a concrete arch dam would work best.

When you grow up, you could be an engineer and plan dams. You could drive a bulldozer and build them. You could even work in a dam's powerhouse and light homes all over town.

Until then, you can
build dams out of sticks
and leaves on a rainy day.

Think about dams next time you get a drink
of water or turn on a light.  Dams store water for
us to use.  They keep us safe from floods.

Dams give us power.

# A Photo Index to the Dams in This Book

**Cover and page 1** Parker Dam fits tightly between the rock walls of a canyon. This kind of dam is called a concrete arch dam. Water from the Colorado River pushes against the concrete arch, pressing the ends of the dam against the canyon wall.

**Page 2** Hoover Dam glows at night. Water flowing through the dam's power-house creates power called hydroelectricity. (*Hydro* means water in Greek.)

**Page 5** Norris Dam holds back the Clinch River in Tennessee. It is a concrete gravity overflow dam. Gravity pulls down on the concrete, holding the dam in place. Water flows over a spillway at the top. The Tennessee Valley Authority built Norris Dam during the Depression. Building the dam gave many people jobs.

**Page 6** Beavers built this dam on the Snake River in Grand Teton National Park in Wyoming. Beavers are nature's great engineers. They change the world around them to make a home.

**Page 7** At 702 feet, Glen Canyon Dam in Arizona is the tallest concrete arch dam in the United States. The dam goes across the Colorado River just upstream from the Grand Canyon.

**Page 8** Nine Mile Creek slips over the top of a dam to make Marcellus Falls in New York State. The dam, built in the early 1900s, replaced an even older dam.

**Page 9** A small dam built of rocks and sticks makes a great place to play. But watch out! Rocks are slippery when they're wet. You might find yourself swimming when you least expect to.

**Page 10** Lake Nasser in Egypt stores water for crops and electricity. The lake, or reservoir, holds water from the Nile River.

**Pages 11 and 12** Hoover Dam is 726 feet tall and 1,244 feet wide. Lake Mead is formed by the Colorado River as it fills the canyon behind the dam. It can hold 12 trillion (that's 12,000,000,000,000) gallons of water! How does water from Lake Mead travel to California? Water goes through the dam's powerhouse and  flows down the Colorado River. At Parker Dam, it passes into the Colorado Aqueduct, a kind of water road. Then canals, tunnels, and pipes carry the water across California. After the water is cleaned, more pipes carry it to homes and backyards all over Los Angeles.

 **Page 13** Lake Mead National Recreation Area covers millions of acres in both Arizona and Nevada.

 **Page 14** The Old Mill in Pigeon Forge, Tennessee, grinds many different grains. Writer David Macaulay shows how old dams and mills were built in his book *Mill*.

 **Page 15** The Bonneville Dam crosses the Columbia River just east of Portland, Oregon. The U. S. Army Corps of Engineers built the concrete gravity overflow dam during the 1930s.

 **Page 16** Pipes called penstocks carry water into a powerhouse. Each penstock leads to a turbine. There are ten turbines inside the powerhouse at Bonneville Dam. Draft tubes under each turbine take the water out of the powerhouse. The tail water bubbles out into the river below.

 **Page 17** Dams along the Columbia River help bring water to dry areas. They make hydroelectricity for much of the Northwest.

 **Page 18** The Bradford Island Fishway helps fish pass around Bonneville Dam. Fish swim upstream to lay their eggs. Then they swim back downstream to find food.

 **Page 19** This scientist is working in the Grand Canyon. The U. S. Fish and Wildlife Service keeps track of the fish in America's rivers. Scientists from environmental groups help, too.

 **Page 20** The floodgates are open! This photograph was taken in April 1996. Water is shooting out below Glen Canyon Dam into the Grand Canyon.

**Page 21** The Gezhouba Dam is one of many dams built to control floods on the Chang River in China. The Chang River is also called the Yangtze River. Both names mean *Long River* in Chinese.

**Page 22** The Thames River flows into the sea. The river has high and low tides, just like the sea. During very high tides, the barrier rises up between hood-shaped posts to hold back water.

**Page 23** Sometimes engineers build a working model of a new dam to test ideas. This kind of model is called a prototype. The dam in this picture is a prototype, built by the Army Corps of Engineers in Smithland, Kentucky. It is a small version of a dam to be built in Olmsted, Illinois.

**Page 24** Crushed stone covers the top of the dam at Lake Arrowhead in California. Earthen dams have stones or grass on the outside. The inside of the dam is made of packed-down dirt.

**Page 25** Rock walls rise up above the Colorado River at Glen Canyon Dam. Engineers tested the rock before they built the dam. The rock proved strong enough to hold the weight of a concrete arch dam.

**Page 26** A worker checks controls at Bonneville Dam. He looks at water levels in the reservoir above the dam and in the tail water below. Would you like to work at a dam?

**Page 27** This girl has a brook near her house where she can build dams. But a gutter on a rainy day is all you really need.

**Page 28** Water rushing over the spillway of Little Goose Dam looks powerful. This dam is on the Snake River in southeastern Washington State.

**Page 29** Fireworks light up the night at Grand Coulee Dam in Washington State.